SINGLE &

Pretty

Breaking Up with Fake Love,
Fake Friends, and the Night Life

I0522120

TIARA BUSTER

ISBN: 979-8-9892806-2-9
120 Publishing House
www.120dayspublishing.com

GET YOUR FREE GIFT!

Hey friend, you are not alone on this journey. I have something just for you! A song that will motivate you on your journey and keep you reminded that there is a way we do things now, and we do them The P.R.E.T.T.Y Way, so click the link below and download a copy of your new favorite song, and tell me what you think!

You can listen by visiting:
shisopretty | Instagram | Linktree

DEDICATION

Hey Pretty Ladies,

I'm Tiara, and I proudly stand as the author of this book. It's still a bit surreal for me, too. Allow me to take a moment to introduce myself properly.

Above all, I consider myself a devoted child of God, driven by a deep love for serving others. I currently reside in the vibrant city of Orlando, Florida, and I'm 35 years young. In addition to my spiritual journey, I also run a beauty business called "ShisoPretty," where I offer a range of services, including eyelash extensions, hair extensions, and eyebrow treatments such as waxing, tinting, and lamination.

For the past eight years, I've proudly carried the mantle of a business owner. However, one day, I received a divine calling from God, one that simply instructed me to write a book. Armed with no more than that directive, I went on this journey, and to my surprise, it unfolded as a reflection of my own experiences over the past decade. It encompassed all the highs and lows that life had thrown my way.

Now, you might be wondering how my personal narrative could possibly be of benefit to you. To this, I can only echo God's words to me: "This book is for you"....

- If you haven't found your purpose
- If you don't know what's next for your life
- If your money is low
- If you don't know your value
- If you don't know what to do with your life
- If your job feels pointless
- If your living life aimlessly
- If you love the night life
- If your thinking about giving up
- If you only pray when you get into trouble
- If you have trouble taking accountability
- If you are giving your body away to guys who don't deserve you

Ladies, it truly is as straightforward as that. My hope and prayer are that as you reach the end of Chapter 9, your spirits will be uplifted, and you'll find yourselves firmly on God's chosen path for your lives.

May God's blessings continue to shower upon each one of you. And hey, if you don't mind, could you do me a favor and give me a follow on Instagram? You can find me at @Tiara_Shisopretty. I'm working on boosting my followers, and your support means a lot. Thank you, and always remember with all that you do, do it "The Pretty Way."

TABLE OF CONTENTS

FOREWORD

From A Purposed and Pretty Mom to her Single and P.R.E.T.T.Y Daughter:

It's not every day that a mother has to pen down a forward to a book written by her own flesh and blood. There's a weight to this task, a weight borne from the shared moments of pain, triumph, despair, and elation. But mostly, it's the weight of a story that I saw unfold before my very eyes. You see, from the depths of the darkest nights, the brightest stars emerge.

In the struggles of my own battles with the night life, drugs, and prison bars, there was a painful void, a chasm that separated me from my family. But this story isn't about my battles; it's about the child who saw it all and grew from the chaos. It's about Tiara.

When you hold this book, *Single and Pretty: Breaking Up with Fake Love, Fake Friends, and the Night Life*, in your hands, you are not merely holding a collection of words; you are cradling the very essence of resilience, love, and the unbreakable spirit of my daughter, Tiara.

From the youngest age, there were hints of the strength within her. At 3, she'd use a rotary phone to call her grandmother and say "come and get me" 😂 –

not an easy feat, mind you. It was a sign, perhaps, of her innate ability to connect, to seek love, and to make her voice heard. At 10, when our house was raided, it was her voice, steady and composed, that kept the wolves of the Child Protection Services at bay. While children her age were consumed with games and innocence, my Tiara was developing the strength of character and the wisdom of someone well beyond her years.

By 13, with me lost in the depths of my own despair, she became the backbone of our family. She not only raised herself but also took upon her young shoulders the responsibility of her siblings. There were times I'd look at her from my own foggy world, and even in my most disillusioned state, I'd think: "She's marked for greatness."

But, there was a letter – *the letter* – that would become the turning point of my life.

One fateful day, a folded piece of paper, an autobiography Tiara had written as part of a scholarship application, landed in my hands. The raw pain, the hope, the unyielding love – every word pierced my heart. It was as if the scales fell from my eyes and I saw, truly saw, the cost of my choices. It was a mirror held up to my soul, and the reflection wasn't flattering. But it was necessary.

After reading that letter, I never touched a drug again. It wasn't an easy journey. The path to redemption is fraught with temptation, guilt, and countless moments of self-doubt. But every time I wavered, I'd think of that letter, and the face of my daughter, and find the strength to move forward.

It's heartwarming to realize that just as Tiara's words pulled me from my darkest and lowest place, this book has the same power to pull its readers from their own personal shadows. Words can heal, and *Single and Pretty* is a testament to that. It serves as a beacon, guiding those entangled in the world of fake love, deceitful friendships, and the blinding lights of the night life.

We are all seeking genuine love, aren't we? In our own missteps and mistakes, in our darkest hours, that's the light we're seeking. And this book? It shows you where to find it. Not in the glitz and glamor, not in the temporary highs, but in the pure, unadulterated love that we all, deep down, yearn for.

Today, our bond, mine and Tiara's, stands as a testimony to the healing power of love, prayer, and faith. There's an unspoken understanding between us, a connection that's almost tangible. During her own battles, it was often my voice, filled with years of experience and genuine concern, that she'd hear, guiding her, comforting her. My prayers for her, our late-night chats – and calls that would come right in the nick of time; they became her armor, shielding her from the world, and even protecting her from opening certain doors that the night life presented.

In many ways, our journey has come full circle. From the small child who watched her mother's descent into darkness to the strong woman who pulled her out from it, Tiara has grown, evolved, and blossomed. I couldn't be prouder. And as you read these pages, I hope you see not just her story, but also the potential of your own redemption, the possibility of finding the light amidst the darkest nights. Don't take a single chapter for granted, because I know that this book was made, just for you!

With love and hope,
Tressa Phillips

INTRODUCTION

Have you ever experienced the weariness of rushing through life at a breakneck pace, only to find that you're not really making any meaningful progress? A decade ago, that was precisely my situation. I was employed in bars and working as a waitress, earning a living and covering my expenses, but my life lacked a sense of purpose. I couldn't help but wonder, "What am I really living for?"

I embarked on a spiritual journey with God. At the age of 27, my faith was solely in God, but I must confess that my intentions were initially somewhat self-serving. I sought God's protection while living a life filled with sin. I wanted to indulge in the thrill of life while under the safety net of God's guidance. I hoped to avoid potential dangers such as kidnapping, drug abuse, and mistreatment.

However, my approach was flawed. By not involving God in my insecurities, self-perception, intimate relationships, partying habits, family dynamics, and friendships, I found myself spiraling downward with no clear direction. I grew weary of avoiding my own reflection, lacking pride in myself, and failing to appreciate the beauty of life. I was exhausted.

It was a turning point when I made the choice to invite God into every facet of my life. His patience and grace astounded me. He waited for my invitation. My love for God deepened immensely. Eight years have passed, and I am a transformed woman, still evolving and continually improving. I am profoundly grateful to Jesus.

Everyone has a story and this is mine.

CHAPTER 1:

Why are you single?

I want to stop giving my body
to men who do not deserve it.

(Bible Verse)
And don't be wishing you were someplace else,
where you are right now is God's place for you. Live
and obey and love and believe right there. God, not
marital status, defines your life. Corinthians 7:17

Have you ever lied to the doctors about the reason why your eye was leaking blood in the emergency room? Well, I have.

Girl, let me tell you about the time I woke up to a black eye and seven stitches on my pretty face.

It all started on a particularly dark and beautiful summer night at a bar in Virginia Beach, Virginia. I was with my roommate and all of a sudden this guy walked in looking so exotic. I mean, curly hair, smooth skin, and a beautiful smile. Cupid must have shot both of us in the ass that night because once we locked eyes we were inseparable. He was Costa Rican with a Spanish accent and the most romantic man I've ever encountered. We talked, we flirted, we held each other and eventually, we locked lips and kissed all night. It was like everyone in the bar disappeared and it was just us two.

As we were leaving the bar we exchanged numbers and that led us to talking for hours on the phone every day which of course led to him asking me to officially become his girlfriend. And of course, I said "Yes". How could I not? I loved him. At that point, because of him, time felt like it slowed down and became more passionate and exciting.

We dated for a while, and it was great. That is, until I invited him to my job at the nightclub, where I got him drunk. I didn't get him drunk on purpose though, it was truly for fun. See, if you know me, then you know I like to have fun. And at that time in my life I was the fun, plus I was the bartender. ☺

Once he left the bar that night, I called and texted him to make sure he was home, but I hadn't received a response; so I got worried. Once I finished my shift and headed to my car, something told me to check the parking garage for his vehicle. And there he was, in his car passed out in the front seat. Of course, as a good girlfriend, I woke him up, helped him get in my vehicle, and as I was fastening his seatbelt, he looked me in the eyes and said

"You came back for me. I love you"

From that moment, I was in love. We were in love. It had gone from great, to the greatest thing ever! We spent all of our free time with each other, and both of our call logs were filled with each other. We also had the best sex, like every time we got together. He took me on my first international trip to Costa Rica to meet his family; which was the best trip of my life, at that point. We also ended up traveling to Michigan so I could introduce him to my family.

Our three-year relationship became stronger than either of us had ever imagined and everything that I could have thought I wanted...

And then he proposed.

Once the ring went on my finger, everything changed. He became very controlling. He would constantly play these mind games by gaslighting me with hopes to make me feel guilty about working in the club and hanging out with my friends and family. Eventually, it worked; he was breaking me down little by little to create an insecure Tiara. I was experiencing psychological and verbal abuse.

However, at the time, I didn't see it as that, because growing up that's all I saw in my household: love, sex, toxicity, and abuse. I thought this was a normal phase in a relationship that everyone experienced. I thought it was an aspect of love that real relationships endured.

I was all in until I found that damn Waffle House receipt in my car 6 months later.

Faked out by Fake Love

One particular night, while I was cooking dinner, he had just come home from work, headed straight to the shower, ate dinner, and then proceeded to head out to the gym for a workout.

This is normal behavior, by the way, so there was no need for me to be alarmed.

So, after about two hours had passed, he returned home and again, headed straight to the shower. As for me, I was studying for my Real Estate exam and realized that I happened to have run out of highlighters. So I slipped on some clothes, grabbed my car keys, and headed to the car. To my surprise, when I got in the car I found a receipt from The Waffle House for two people that was time-stamped to the time my fiancé was supposed to be at the gym.

Now I'm confused.

I head to the nearest store and purchase the highlighters then head right back home. However, before immediately going into the house, I stayed in the car trying to figure out how I was going to ask this man "Why would he go to The Waffle House and eat when I just fed him when he got home from work?"

Fuck it! I needed to know NOW! Because I know he did not have another female in MY car.

"Hey Bae, how was The Waffle House?"

His response "What are you talking about?"

Before I knew it, I'm pinned up in the corner trying to fight my way out.

It's important to know that this is not the first fight we've had at this point. Therefore, I know how far this can go and how long this was going to be. All night!

Well, all of a sudden, amid all the fighting, my phone began to ring. As I tried to reach for the phone inside my pocket, he knocked it out of my hand and it flew across the floor but I was able to recognize the screen to know it was my mom calling. Call it what you want, but my mom KNEW something was wrong with her child (I'll label it extrasensory perception). He looked at me and then looked at the phone and we both ran for it like it was a fumble on the play in an intense football game.

Eventually, I blacked out and as I was regaining consciousness, I noticed blood everywhere, and all I heard was "Baby I'm sorry! Baby, I'm sorry"

This man, my fiancé, the man who I loved and wanted to have a future with, pushed me out of the way so hard that I could not retrieve my cell phone that my head hit the window seal and split my eyebrow open. I was so light-headed and weak that all I could do was beg him to take me to the emergency room.

Upon arriving at the emergency room, because my bleeding was so severe I was seen immediately. The nurses were suspicious and started giving me the third degree as to what happened. Every fiber in my body wanted to tell them to call the police and that he pushed me, but he never left my side. So I lied and said "I slipped out of the shower".

Love is blind and it will take over your fucking mind. Love will have you looking stupid, scared, and lost...at least for me it did. But enough was enough, one look at my face that next morning and all I could see was...my mother.

Growing up, I watched my mother go through an abusive relationship with a man who claimed he loved her. From the infatuation and public displays of affection to the constant arguments, to the screaming and actual fist fighting, the cycle of abuse was something I knew all too well. Since I'm being honest, from a young age, that shit used to irritate the hell out of me; so much that I would hide in the closet and pray to God that He would stop the fighting and save my mom.

It was at that moment, that reality hit and I knew that I had to get away and go somewhere that my fiancé couldn't find me.

Immediately after that thought, the next thought was me moving to Florida.

Orlando, Florida to be exact.

Orlando was the place my ex-Russian boyfriend, (the boyfriend before my Costa Rican finance) used to always take me to visit. He had friends that worked in the Medieval Times Dinner & Tournament Events, you know, with all the horses and shows? So I was familiar with the city and had always told myself that Florida was going to be the next state I'd move to.

So I made a plan:

1. **Get a second job,**
2. **Save up 6 months of rent**
3. **Set a moving date**
4. **Leave**

My family wasn't too happy about my "all of a sudden" plans, but I couldn't explain at the time what was leading me to move to Florida. But four months later, I packed up my honda accord front to back and I never looked back.

Now when someone asks me why I'm single, I tell them because I choose to be. My life is simple, peaceful, and productive, and I am so happy.

***

100%  THE PRETTY WAY

Recognizing the beauty and excellence in everything around you and within you.

Single & Pretty Protip: Unconditional Love

INGREDIENTS:

You deserve to feel the same love that you give. Love can come in many forms, such as romantic love, familial love, platonic love, & self-love. Here are some great ways to express your love.

Recycle

QUALITY TIME   PHYSICAL AFFECTION   EXPRESS APPRECIATION   LISTEN ACTIVELY   BE SUPPORTIVE

CHAPTER 2:

Aimlessly Living

I had to eliminate my distractions
and find my purpose.

(Bible Verse)
Keep your eyes straight ahead, and ignore all
sideshow distractions. Proverbs 4:25

Your ability to overcome distraction will be the number one determinant of how successful you are on your path to purpose.

You can give your distractions all kinds of names, but the main ones that come to mind are fear, pleasure, pain, lust, worry, and procrastination.

- **Fear** - scared of the unknown or change. Staying stuck in the same living situation, relationship, or job just because you're afraid of the outcome.
- **Pleasure** - an emotional feeling of enjoyment. Too much of the "feel good" dopamine released in the brain can cause addictive behaviors :(ie gambling, drugs, food addictions, sex).
- **Pain** - an unpleasant feeling that causes distress and suffering. When you are hurt internally you will feel dissatisfied and empty, like life has no meaning.
- **Lust** - a strong sexual desire for the flesh. Fantasizing over someone's body parts instead

of the whole person is a form of sexual objectification.

- **Worry** - constant hypothetical thoughts that can cause anxiety. It can make you live in a constant state of fight-or-flight alertness.
- **Procrastination** - delaying the things that you're supposed to do. It can keep you stagnant in your growth process throughout life.

Anything that pulls our attention away from God is a distraction.

My so-called "friends" were my biggest distraction.

You know the friends you meet at work or in social circles that make all the bad decisions in life seem like the most exciting, free, YOLO-experiencing moments you needed to partake in to live? Yeah...them.

I don't know about you, but I wanted to experience it. I needed it. I was new to Orlando and secured a new job and a new apartment. I was living a new life. The city was welcoming me with open arms. I was ready to live!

I had no plan once I got there. I've never been much of a planner. I was more like the "go with the flow" kind of person even though my mature intuition and critical thinking skills have always partnered together to keep me out of danger and propel me into making the wisest decisions for my life.

So there I was, aimlessly living my best life in the beautiful sunny state of Florida, basking in the reality of a fresh start and what did I do? Hustle.

My main job was working as a Timeshare Agent at Wyndham Bonnet Creek Resort and my second job was part-time store associate at Victoria's Secret in the Millenia Mall. The hustle didn't stop there though, my third job was my all-time favorite – waitressing at one of the pillars of the city, the Corona Cigar Company, the downtown location. It was the gathering spot for the NBA ball players, doctors, lawyers, entertainers, golfers, and every type of businessman with money. And I made A LOT of money catering to those businessmen with their cognac and cigars. Once I learned the hustle, I was headed for the top. All I had to do was wear a little sexy black dress, keep a smile on my face at all times, remember their drink order, and know how to assist with clipping the cigar and lighting it if asked. My pockets were loaded every time I worked.

However, my biggest hustle came from my job as a Timeshare Agent. Now this one took a lot and

I mean a lot of practice, repetition, and then even more practice. But once I got my pitch down, I was on fire. I started getting sales and making money, like real money. We got paid monthly, but the checks were so fat all I wanted to do was go shopping for better clothes and shoes. Fashion was a necessity, in Orlando, you had to look like money to get more money.

The downside to it all was, I was not good with money management because I was spending it as fast as I was making it. And one thing they don't tell you about when becoming a Timeshare Agent is that it's only 3-4 months a year that you can make a living. June through September are the money-making months, and if you are surviving after that, you either have a second job that pays more or a spouse to help with bills.

It was all good until I caught one of the managers and another sales agent teaming up to steal my deal so they could hit the top bonus that month. If the fire in my eyes was a person, I'd still be in a jail cell to this day.

But thank God for Human Resources.

You see ladies, Human Resources should be your best friend. If utilized correctly you can have power or it can be used against you to make you powerless. Once I reported them, I had the power, and shit got real. Long story short, they were terminated and I got transferred to another department because I was curious about the operational side of the company. Plus, that was where all the real money and desired stability were.

A couple of months into my new position, I met a girl who I thought was so cool and like me, loved going out. We would go downtown and live life to the fullest. The bars were our favorite place to meet up and when we did we always got drunk. And as a part of our night-out routine, I would just crash at her place since she lived a couple of blocks from the bars downtown.

On our days off we would meet up at my place and day drink at the pool. This became our lifestyle pattern for about 6 to 8 months. That is until one day in January, I was arrested and taken to the Orlando County Jail.

I was pulled over around 8 pm right after my friend and I had gotten done partying for the night.

Yes, I was arrested and charged with Driving Under the Influence of Alcohol (DUI).

Fear was never an emotional trait I've expressed, but embarrassment was. All I could think about was what my coworkers would think and the fact that I couldn't call anyone because I was too ashamed.

So I called a bail bondsman.

Once I was charged and released from jail I was given a court date that I needed to secure a lawyer for. At this point, I was fresh out of ideas and solutions, and so ashamed to tell anyone that I was arrested and needed money for my DUI. I didn't know what to do. All I wanted to do was hide and stay hidden, but life doesn't work like that, Sis.

Once I got home and showered, I got on my knees and started praying,

"Heavenly Father, I am so sorry. I repent for all the sins I committed. I don't know when or where I lost focus, but I need you now. My lawyer is $2,500 and the DUI classes are expensive too. Lord, please help me. In Jesus' name, Amen."

Well, my court date arrived and I was placed in the pretrial diversion program which allows offenders to have their DUI charge reduced to reckless driving.

I was given a list of fines that must be paid in full, if not there would be a warrant issued for my arrest, and I would be locked up, again. The judge also ordered me to attend DUI school and victim impact classes while also committing to random urine screenings. It didn't stop there either because I also had to complete over 80 hours in Alcoholics Anonymous and along with other counseling sessions. Oh, and my car? I had to get the ignition interlock device installed in my vehicle for 6 months.

The whole process lasted a full year and it was indeed the most strenuous process of my life. However, the discipline, knowledge of self, courage, and faith I achieved throughout the process was a blessing from God. My life was never the same after that incident.

That night specifically is what some will call a paradigm shift. A paradigm shift is defined as an important change that happens when the usual way of thinking about something is replaced by a new and different way.

What was I doing?

I had no vision. I had no goals. I was just aimlessly living.

You see, living life aimlessly will get you wrapped up in all kinds of social settings: nightlife, sex, parties, drugs, crime, stripping, and much more. And after all that partying, traveling, drinking, and sex you're having, how do you feel?

How does your soul feel?

Are you tired of waking up hungover wondering what happened last night or if you posted something on social media that could have the office gossiping about you at work?

Or maybe you're tired of wondering if your sneaky link might have taken off the condom without your knowledge when it was getting good and now you're wondering if you should just go get the Plan B pill just in case?

Believe me, I've been there.

You see all the things I described above are called distractions. They are distracting you from your purpose. When you are gifted with life, God gives us all purpose to serve.

Also, from the time you were born, The Enemy, Satan, job is to distract you from your purpose. Now how do you get rid of him is the question. I started by using simple steps that I had control over.

Have you ever heard of fasting?

Fasting is a spiritual discipline that is taught in the Bible. It is to voluntarily reduce or eliminate your intake of food for a specific time and purpose. However, eliminating food for forty days was not recommended by my physician because of my anemia. So I prayed about it and God gave me an idea:

- Take 3 bad habits you currently have in your life and remove them for 40 days
- Take 3 good habits that will better your life and add them for 40 days

For example:

That DUI changed my life.

God had to get my attention somehow. Usually, a good indicator to know when God is sending you signals to slow down is when He sends friendly fire. For example, since moving to Orlando, I have been drugged twice. I still don't know what they put in my drink, but for whatever reason I would wake up in my bed the next day completely unaware of what had happened the night before.

WOW Tiara, if that wasn't a sign then what was?

You see, as I mentioned earlier, the further you are away from God the less you can hear His voice. I would always feel like something was after me, but I was living my life so deep in the flesh and when The Devil has your ear he will double down to make sure you're under his full submission.

Babe, I was almost there, but God.

He came and got me. You see God knows His children. He will hand you a rope long enough that when you start to tug, He reels you in and right into His arms.

Pride will bury you and shame will keep you buried. But when you humble yourself you will start to position your heart in the direction God has for us. God is always there, waiting in the shadows ready to come and rescue you. And that's just what He did.

I had to take a good look at myself and my actions and ask God to give me the right view of myself as He sees me. That night in my dream, I saw this beautiful woman in a house that she turned into a spa that was decorated so nicely. She was well respected and a leader that spoke with young girls around the world about never giving up on yourself, no matter how difficult the upbringing.

That woman became my goal.

Subsequently, my DUI lawyer was paid for and my charges were reduced to reckless driving. I am actively leading by example for the women in my family and my peers by letting God guide me and speak through me.

That's it, ladies, it's that simple. Oh, and that 40-day fast has been my yearly ritual twice a year for over 6 years now. The blessings and spiritual guidance you will receive from the discipline you display to honor God will change your life forever.

100%

PRETTY

THE PRETTY WAY

Recognizing the beauty and excellence in everything around you and within you.

Single & Pretty Protip: Set Boundaries for yourself

INGREDIENTS:

Boundaries are limits we set for ourselves and other in order to establish a sense of safety, security, and respect in relationships and interactions with people.

Recycle

EMOTIONAL BOUNDARIES   MENTAL BOUNDARIES   PHYSICAL BOUNDARIES   SELF RESPECT   SAY NO

CHAPTER 3:

Celibacy

I need to stop messing with
f*ck boys and have control
over my hormones.

(Bible Verse)
For everything in the world– the lust of the flesh,
the lust of the eyes, and the pride of life– comes not
from God, but from the world.
1 John 2:16

Being sexually active with guys I was not in a relationship with left me feeling ugly, internally and externally. I would look in the mirror and think,

"You must be ugly because he's not calling you back"

"He keeps inviting you to places with no intentions of actually taking you, what's wrong with you?"

"I don't know why he only calls after midnight, and I always pick up."

This was the treatment I received from guys until one day I made the decision with God and myself that I was no longer going to tolerate that kind of treatment.

A part of this treatment came about because I lacked self-worth which was proven by how reckless I was with my sex life. And I mean reckless. SO reckless that when I would meet a guy in the club, we would have a good time and he would buy me drinks; that automatically qualified him to have sex with me. Mind you, that would be without me knowing his last name, or sexual status (meaning if he had an STD) - that's the part that made me cringe and say to myself,

"Tiara, do you care about your life"?

Eventually, I became disgusted with myself and realized that if I wanted to see change, I had to be the change and work on myself.

So what did I do? I STOPPED having sex.

In February 2016, Celibacy, the personal decision to abstain from sexual activity, became my next journey. I made a vow to myself and God that I would not have sex for the next 40 days.

During the beginning of my celibacy journey, I began to take accountability for my risky lifestyle. It was then that I quickly realized how dangerous it was to give my body to a man without any allegiance to me. Not only could it affect my physical body along with my mind, emotions, and self-worth - but I could've birthed a whole human being because of it.

Then what?

My life would've drastically changed forever because of that quick moment of pleasure. I could've been a mother sooner than I intended and forced to co-parent with a man who may or may not have stepped up to his parental obligations.

I wanted more for my life than that.

***

My next focus was my physical health. Engaging in unprotected casual sex puts me at risk of contracting sexually transmitted infections (STIs) such as chlamydia, gonorrhea, herpes, HPV, and HIV. Some of these infections can have serious long-term consequences, such as infertility and even certain types of cancer. However, using condoms can help reduce the risk of STIs...and that's where I fucked up.

As my journey went on, I can say that one of the benefits of my not being sexually active was that I studied the anatomy of my body. Meaning, since I was no longer having sex, I could learn how my hormones and the bacteria that I was exposing myself to via sex, affected me good and bad.

I explored what caused me to get yeast infections and bacterial vaginosis (BV). I learned that it could have been the condom, raw sex, his bacteria and mines not aligning, or even the thongs I would wear.

As a result, bad hygiene and body odor became my main focus. Some certain signs and symptoms will alert us about poor hygiene practices. Vaginal odor is the one that says you're not paying proper attention to your vagina. Foul smells and discharge should be the first signal to yourself that you need to see a doctor asap. Not peeing after sex will cause urinary tract infections. Your body needs to flesh out the bacteria.

And omg the itching that came from a yeast infection was so irritating. Frequent doctor visits would scare the hell out of me. But now being able to finally honestly answer the question of how many sex partners have you had in the past 6 months when asked by the doctor and a negative lab test gave me so much joy. Zero– would fly out my mouth so fast, with so much confidence. Knowing your sex count is a serious thing and not knowing or lying about the actual number is a part of low self-esteem.

Casual sex doesn't just affect your physical health but it seeps into your mental health as well. While some girls may feel empowered and fulfilled, other girls may feel guilty or regretful afterward.

Sex used to make me feel empowered when I was in a relationship. When I made love to my man we would experience intense sensations throughout our bodies. Intimacy was our love language that created closeness and vulnerability. Sex outside of a relationship slowly chipped away at my soul. Immediately after having sex with a random guy, I was regretful. It would make my skin crawl when the guy would get up and leave and I get ghosted after. Ugh, what was I thinking... Sometimes I still can't believe that was my life for about two years. I'm glad I didn't have a long run of a hoe phase because I was engaging in more sexual activity than normal. It made me feel conflicted and unsure about my choices, especially because I was not receiving the emotional connection or validation I was accustomed to.

It's important to note that everyone's emotional response to casual sex is unique and valid. And while there is no "right" or "wrong" way to feel, you should be mindful of how it will affect your self-esteem and self-worth because it will; especially if you engage in it for the wrong reasons, such as seeking validation or acceptance.

How can you tell if you're into casual sex for the wrong reasons?

Ask yourself, "How do I feel when a guy ejaculates and the sex is over?"

If your spirit, not your hormones, but your spirit feels empty because you both have no substance with each other then you should consider making celibacy your first choice to being single and pretty.

While celibacy focuses on sexual discipline, it can also be a way to prioritize your personal growth and healing, or it can be a way to avoid intimacy and vulnerability, which can be a sign of deeper issues that may require therapy or other forms of support.

It has now been 7 wonderful years of celibacy for me. Who knew that abstaining from sex would bring me clarity, job promotions, independence, financial stability, my first house, and a growing business? But with prayer, celibacy, and discipline I got my beauty back.

Taking time for yourself is a necessity for your life. Learning discipline for your sex life helps train our mind and body which allows us to focus on our goals, regulate our emotions, and maintain our mental health.

Ultimately, it's up to you to decide whether celibacy is an important part of your journey. If you do decide to remain celibate, it is important to communicate your boundaries clearly to potential partners and to practice self-care and self-compassion. Remember that your worth is not determined by your sexual activity or lack thereof and that you deserve to be respected and valued for who you are as a person.

100%
PRETTY

THE PRETTY WAY

Recognizing the beauty and excellence in everything around you and within you.

Single & Pretty Protip: The Power of "NO"

INGREDIENTS:

Saying "NO" is empowering, because it allows you to prioritize your own needs and values, rather than acquiescing to the demands of others.

Recycle

CLEAR BOUNDARIES

AVOID OVER-COMMITTING

MAINTAIN CONTROL OVER YOUR TIME

POLITELY SAY NO

AVOID UNNECESSARY CONFLICTS

CHAPTER 4:

Place God at the center
of your life

Make God your love interest

(Bible Verse)
In everything you do, put God first, and he will direct
you and crown your efforts with success.
Proverbs 3:6

Your family has the biggest influence on your overall development, whether they are conscious of it or not. Biblically speaking, we inherit the generational pattern of sins from our family, which is why it's good to study and know your family history. If not, it will continue to negatively affect your life and the lives of those you birth and love.

Knowing what I know about my family history, I pride myself on setting boundaries for my life so that I don't fall into the same traps as my parents and even my grandparents. You see, I stem from a family who has formed generational curses for me.

Generational curses are sins, misdeeds, or negative actions passed down to future generations from our ancestors.

In my family, my grandmother and my grandfather both spent time in prison and struggled with drugs at a point in their lives. However, it became a generational curse when my mother and father had to spend a portion of their lives in prison, and struggled with the same drugs that my grandparents struggled with.

Today, I am grateful and blessed to say that everyone is home and drug-free. Except for my grandmother, who passed away from an asthma attack when I was a senior in high school.

I am also grateful that, under the protection of God, I have broken the cycle of prison and drug abuse for my family.

John 8:31-36 reminds us that as we aid in Jesus Christ, we receive His freedom. He is the burden-removing, yoke-destroying power of God who lives inside us.

***

I remember getting baptized at the age of seven. I also remember getting baptized at eight years old... and then again at nine years old. Everyone was getting baptized when they turned 10, so I was baptized then too. Oh! and then again at thirty-three. Huh, I guess you could call me a "serial baptizer" because if it was happening, I was in line. But when I reflect on my life and focus on my upbringing it was and still is a normal feeling of mine to be in God's presence. It was the only place I could run to as a kid and feel safe. Whenever I was frightened, unsure, worried, or confused I would seek Him. No matter what my situation was, I knew God would comfort me and make a way. It was like I had this shield of protection over me that I couldn't physically see or feel, but I felt it in my spirit. Bible scholars would call it "God's covering" or spiritual protection in which God provides for those who are in a covenant relationship with Him. There were times when I would test that notion and pray for things, only to see if God could hear me and whether He would keep his promises.

And He always did.

Let me tell you a secret, if you fuck with me, mean me any bad will, harm, or misdirection for my life— God has a history of drastically intervening on my behalf and it was never pretty. I've watched Him do it several times throughout my lifetime, which also confirms to me that I am a child of God.

Can you look back on your life and see when, where, and how God has rescued you or come to your defense?

Growing up, my biological father wasn't around much to help my mother with the day-to-day parenting; mainly because he was sent to prison when I was 8 years old and stayed there until I was 14 years old. Out of duty, or maybe hope for better days, we would write letters to one another on the holidays and birthdays. If you've ever received a card or letter from someone, more specifically a parent, in prison you know that promises will be made, dreams will be sold, and hearts will be broken. And at that time, 8-12-year-old Tiara believed any and everything that came out of the mouth of adults. Because that's what we were supposed to do, right? Trust them?

Yeah, well that didn't last for too long.

My father was released from prison when I was 12 years old and was sentenced right back 19 days after he was released. How could a father who loves his daughter, promise her trips, movies, amusement parks, and outings, and within 19 days of his freedom commit another crime that gets him sentenced to another 2 years in prison?

That was my first heartbreak.

That's when I stopped being naive and realized that adults can be liars and that I couldn't trust people based on what they said. Your actions and your words should always agree with each other. That was the first lesson I taught myself and I made an agreement with myself to always do what I say I will do.

Coping and moving on from that experience was rough for me and took a lot of time, years even. And then, while dealing with that trauma, my mom somehow connected with a man and started using drugs.

They say "A man can fuck your life up if you let him"...and my mom let him.

My mom was and still is one of the prettiest women in Muskegon, Michigan and I remember her dating lots of men. Her favorite phrase was "Don't put all your eggs in one basket."

(Translation: Always have someone on the side so when the relationship is over, you don't want to be left all alone and broke.)

I understand what she meant. Hell, she was on her third child with one baby daddy in prison and the other one on drugs. So like most single moms, if you put all your eggs, meaning time and money in one basket, you will be broke and most likely homeless.

Not my mom, she was different, she was a hustler. A natural-born hustler. Literally. She always kept a job at the nursing home or the hospital. But I guess there was a time when the money wasn't coming in fast enough for her, so the new hustle became selling drugs. Long story short, she became a victim of "getting high on your supply".

My mom would be gone for weeks without saying a word to us. And then there was me, the oldest of three siblings. My brother was 10, my sister was 2, and I at 12, automatically and naturally I assumed the responsibility of the caretaker.

The second mother.

I got up early every morning before school to make sure they ate breakfast, were dressed, and were ready to be picked up by my uncle who went around and picked up all the kids for school in his van. It was months before my family found out what was going on inside of our home but once they did, my siblings and I were split up and taken from our home to other family members' homes to be cared for.

That was my first experience with embarrassment. However, I remember the relief I felt because I knew I kept my mothers secret for way too long.

While those years were tough for me, they were also pivotal because that is when God started to do mighty things in my life. While my mother and father were going through the world's sinking hole, God was building me, strengthening me, molding me, and protecting me.

***

You see, life has a funny way of rearing its head. While I was separated from my parents and siblings, God took me through a process that took years for me to see the light at the end of the tunnel.

I was learning to adapt to different households, experiencing how to live with other people, being "seen but not heard", and becoming a great cleaner (because everyone loves a clean house...but mainly so they will think twice before kicking me out), and spending time alone with God.

Yes, there were discouraging times when I asked God,

"Why did my life turn out like this at such a young age?"

"Why my parents, God?"

There were also times when I felt as if I did something to disappoint God and he was punishing me. But I learned that's not how God works. He was perfecting me through the struggle.

But despite how I felt and what I battled mentally, you could never tell because I was determined to not look like what I was going through. Even though the odds and statistics were against me, I never became a disrespectful kid and I always honored my parents no matter how I felt and what they did. And still, to this day, I am receiving the blessings.

Many religious and spiritual traditions teach that the struggles of life are an essential part of our spiritual growth and development. These struggles can take many forms, including illness, loss, financial difficulties, and relationship problems. Through these struggles, we can learn important lessons about ourselves and our place in the world. These lessons have the potential to teach and develop us into a more compassionate, patient, and understanding person. They can also teach us to rely on our faith or spirituality for comfort and strength during difficult times.

God uses these struggles to shape us into the people we are meant to be. Just as a sculptor chips away a block of stone to reveal the beauty within, God uses the struggles of life to refine us and help us become our best selves.

I know not everyone believes in God or subscribes to religious teachings. However, many people find comfort and meaning in the idea that their struggles serve a greater purpose and can ultimately help them grow and evolve as individuals.

100%

PRETTY

THE PRETTY WAY

Recognizing the beauty and excellence in everything around you and within you.

Single & Pretty Protip:
GOD-FIDENCE

INGREDIENTS:

Your mind will believe everything you tell it. So feed it faith, feed it truth, and feed it love. Faith on God will provide a profound sense of peace and security, enabling you to face challenges with courage and resilience.

Recycle

POWER   GUIDANCE   FAITH   COURAGE   RESILIENCE

CHAPTER 5:

Rejoicing in Adversity

Smile through the hate

(Bible Verse)
Trust the Lord with all your heart; do not depend
on your understanding. Seek His will in all you do,
and he will show you which path to take. Don't be
impressed with your own wisdom. Instead, fear the
Lord and turn away from evil. - Proverbs 3:5-7

Let me be clear, I don't want to make it seem like getting my shit together was easy at all. As if, writing goals in the mirror and the Law of Attraction was the solution to fixing all the bullshit I created for myself. Having sex without standards, driving drunk, engaging in gossip, lacking self-esteem, and living life aimlessly had me out on these streets looking crazy.

When life forced me to sit in silence with myself, I became aware of how much my pride was negatively affecting my life. I found myself circling the same circumstance year after year, boyfriend after boyfriend, job after job, and apartment after apartment, taking two steps forward only to take 10 steps back. It was blinding me from seeing my growth opportunities and I got to a point where I was tired of it. Tired of myself. Tired of having my pride leading me to failure. I was TIRED chile.

The crazy thing is, out of all the people I was engaging in these activities with, nobody was willing to correct me or call me out on all my bullshit, they just smiled in my face and talked about me behind my back. My first lesson was to accept responsibility for the outcomes of the decisions I made. That's called accountability, which looks like admitting when you've made a mistake and taking the right steps to make amends. It might involve being transparent with your intentions and even communicating openly and honestly to others.

My next lesson was learning that in times of transition, you have to "keep it tight". That is, keeping your mind tight, keeping your money tight, keeping your circle of friends tight, and keeping your social media usage tight. Please note that whenever God is working in you and through you, the enemy (devil) will always try to sabotage it by tempting you with actions that are contrary to God's plan. This may manifest as negative thoughts, circumstances, or people that seek to hinder your progress toward the good things that God has in store for you. However, through prayer, faith, and your trust in God, you can overcome the devil's attempts to distract you. So keep it tight and stay ready!

***

My favorite bible verse I love to recite for comfort and facing challenges is "No weapon formed against me will prosper". It reminds me that I am not alone and that I have the strength and protection of God on my side. Meaning, no matter what obstacles I may face, they can be overcome with the help of God.

But girl, the weapons...they formed! As soon as I decided to change my life, the haters and distractions were in full effect. They were there trying to discourage me, spreading rumors and lies about me, and actively working to sabotage all of my efforts. Remember the word friend I used to go out drinking with in Chapter 2? Yes, her. She spread rumors that I was sleeping with a manager at work, which was a bald-faced lie because I was practicing celibacy during that time. While I didn't understand why she would say something like that, now I know it was because I was no longer that drunk wild girl that she was used to me being. Because of the restrictions from my DUI, I was not drinking anymore, which allowed me to have a clear mind to focus on growing within the company and staying out of trouble.

I was growing and glowing babe, and that just didn't sit right with her.

She even told me one day that I changed, so much so, that whenever I would come around her at work she would walk away. Long story short, she was fired a couple of months later. I look at it as God moving her out of my way.

She wasn't my only hater though, I also had a supervisor that would try to write me up for things that I was not a part of because she was threatened by my potential within the company. Once she saw the new manager taking a liking to me and all the overtime I was receiving she became determined to speed-track me out of the company through disciplinary write-ups. Little did she know, every single one of the accusations she tried to submit to upper management was denied, due to the personal relationships I had formed with the higher-ups. They didn't believe her and long story short she was also fired and I gained a promotion. God moved her out of my way as well.

Shortly after that was when I learned my next lesson - realizing that it wasn't the enemy that was sending these people on my path, it was God testing my character.

He was testing my faith to see if He could use me.

See, God's test can take various forms, such as adversity, temptation, and suffering which can be used as opportunities for you to learn important lessons and gain wisdom. How you respond to the challenges will reveal your true character and level of faith, and will lead you to spiritual growth and development. Regardless of the nature and purpose of the test, you should view it as an opportunity to deepen your relationship with God, trust His plan, and develop a sense of resilience and perseverance.

Let me break it down even more for you:

You are going to face haters who will aim to try to stop you from pursuing your goals; that's why it's important to stay focused. Don't let their negativity distract you, instead surround yourself with positive, supportive people who will encourage you. If the haters have a valid criticism, use it constructively to improve yourself or your work. But above all, believe in yourself and your abilities. Don't let the haters make you doubt yourself or your worthiness to achieve your goals.

100% THE PRETTY WAY

Recognizing the beauty and excellence in everything around you and within you.

Single & Pretty Protip: Smile More

INGREDIENTS:

Believe it or not, smiling is the best nonverbal way to communicate to others that you are a happy person and approachable.

Recycle

| UPLIFT SOMEONE'S SPIRIT | MEET NEW PEOPLE | ERASE NEGATIVE THOUGHTS | CHANGES THE MOOD | SMILING IS CONTAGIOUS |

CHAPTER 6:

Strong Holds

Go deeper and reap the reward

(Bible Verse)
"No weapon formed against me will prevail."
Isaiah 54:17

Amid all the tests and character development, my dreams became more and more lucid, it was like I could feel my life changing in real time. I remember waking up every morning and meditating for 10 - 20 minutes seeking God's presence regularly ... then one day I had a vision.

My vision was of me doing eyelash extensions.

Now this was mind-blowing to me because I had been applying eyelash extensions on myself and my family since I was 14 years old, but I never even thought about applying them on strangers. I didn't even realize it was possible to start a business applying eyelashes. The vision didn't make sense to me at all, but I could feel that was the direction God was leading me to.

So without a business name or an LLC, I began working on my eyelash business. My focus was simply on perfecting my craft. My first investment was a $100 training kit from Amazon. Then I began watching

Youtube videos all night to research different techniques I could learn. I then took it a step further and spent 3 hours every day after work practicing applying lash extensions on a mannequin head. After 99 practice applications, I met the nicest lady who was willing to certify me in her eyelash extension course for a reasonable price. After the completion of that course, I took it another step further and found an esthetician school that also accepted me for a reasonable price.

It was insane how everything was aligning so perfectly for me...until I faced my next obstacle. I didn't have the schedule for me to work full-time and attend school.

"It's only 24 hours in a day Tiara", I thought, "How will this work?"

...and then I watched God work!

While I was in my weekly scheduled meeting with my manager, I explained to her that I wanted to start my own eyelash business and that it was difficult for me to attend esthetician school because my class hours were during work hours. Without having to expound any further, she responded with "Use the mornings for your school and come to work after".

Who?

What?

How?

It had to be God working through her, working through me. That's the only explanation I could rationalize in my brain. But I took her advice and began attending esthetician school in the morning and reported to work right after. I became even more focused on my dreams and the immense power I started receiving from God was so revitalizing that no one was able to sidetrack me. When office gossip was becoming a problem, without even asking, my manager created an office space for me to be isolated from the rest of the office. She needed me to focus and I needed me to remain focused.

Once I was licensed and certified, one of my trainees helped me get my LLC, my co-worker gifted me with a professional esthetician bed, the IT guy at work helped me with my logo and referred me to my current payroll accountant, and another co-worker helped me with all my merchandise and marketing needs. All the people I worked with daily, helped me get everything together for my business. Thank you, God!

While everything seemed to be coming together seamlessly, starting and growing a business was the most challenging experience for me. I was a pro on the mannequin head but scared as hell to do professional work on someone I didn't know and let alone get paid for it. I had a tough time believing that God put me in the presence of everyone I needed to know to help me get my business out of my head and turn it into reality.

And that, ladies, is called Imposter Syndrome.

Imposter syndrome is a psychological phenomenon characterized by persistent feelings of inadequacy, self-doubt, and fear of being exposed as a fraud or an imposter, despite evidence of competence, success, or achievements. It causes many entrepreneurs to doubt their abilities, question their decisions, and feel like they are not qualified or experienced enough to succeed.

Some common feelings associated with imposter syndrome when starting and growing a business might include:

- Feeling like a fraud or an imposter, even when you have a successful business
- Believing that you are not qualified or skilled enough to run a business

- Fearing that others will discover that you are not as competent or knowledgeable as you appear
- Discounting your achievements or successes, attributing them to luck or other external factors
- Feeling anxious or overwhelmed by the challenges of running a business
- Struggling to make decisions, second-guessing yourself, and procrastinating
- Avoiding risk or opportunities because you fear failure or rejection

To overcome imposter syndrome, you have to acknowledge and challenge your negative self-talk and limiting beliefs. You can also get support from mentors, peers, or a therapist who can offer guidance and help you gain a new perspective on your strengths and weaknesses. Additionally, focusing more on learning and growth, setting realistic goals, and celebrating small successes along the way can help you build confidence and as a result, reduce imposter syndrome.

As for me, staying focused, and eliminating distractions helped change my perspective to the realization that God was keeping me covered. It wasn't about being popular with my friends and colleagues anymore, it was about allowing God to use and groom me so that I could handle the next stage that He wanted me to go to. It was a part of the process to see what I could ultimately handle and develop me to eventually handle what I currently couldn't.

It's important to know that God is not going to give us something that causes us to take a step back from who He is. So He says, "Let me test them to see if I can give them what I ordained for them to have or to see if they will get so big that they will forget who I am."

***

I found that living by these principles can help you deepen your connection with God and will eventually lead you to live a fulfilling spiritual life.

- **Faith:** Having faith in God and trusting His plan is an important principle of following

God. Believers often turn to prayer, scripture, and other spiritual practices to strengthen their faith and deepen their connection to God.

- **Obedience:** Following God requires obedience to His commands and teachings. This includes obeying His Word by living a moral and ethical life while treating others with love and compassion.

- **Humility:** Acknowledging that God is all-knowing and all-powerful and that we are imperfect and fallible, is an important principle of following God. This involves recognizing our weaknesses and limitations and seeking God's guidance and wisdom.

- **Service:** Serving others and doing good works is often seen as an important part of following God. This can involve volunteering, donating to charity, and helping those in need.

- **Forgiveness:** Forgiving others and seeking forgiveness for our own mistakes and shortcomings is a key principle of following God. This involves letting go of grudges and resentments and striving to live a life of love and compassion.

- **Love:** Loving God and loving others are often seen as the foundation of following God. This involves treating others with kindness and respect and striving to live a life of compassion and empathy.

***

Overcoming strongholds in life, and in business, requires God's guidance and involves relying on His wisdom. As you reflect on your own life and business, seek to identify the challenges or obstacles that are hindering your success and then pray for God's guidance. Ultimately, the goal is for you to trust in God's plan for your life and surrender control to Him. Don't worry! His wisdom will lead you in the right direction to live a purpose-driven life.

100%

THE PRETTY WAY

Recognizing the beauty and excellence in everything around you and within you.

Single & Pretty Protip: "Manifestation"

INGREDIENTS:
Say it with me: "I am about to walk into the most successful & soul-nourishing year of my life."

The secret is once you've decided what you want, you should visualize that desire, release all thoughts of fear, and believe in your ability to manifest.

Recycle

| DECIDE WHAT YOU WANT | VISUALIZE YOUR DESIRE | RELEASE LIMITING BELIEFS | TAKE ACTION | ALLOW THE PROCESS TO UNFOLD |

CHAPTER 7:

Get Busy

How can you be pretty when
you're stressed about finances?

(Bible Verse)
"Keep your thoughts continually fixed on all that is
authentic, honorable and admirable, beautiful and
respectful, pure and holy, merciful and kind. And
fasten your thoughts on every glorious work of God,
praising him always."- Phillippians 4:8

A sober mind is a motherf*cker!

Remember that dream I mentioned earlier in the book? The one about my future and how I would become an esthetician? Yes, that one. I saw my future life so clearly that it scared me. But instead of ignoring the dream, I got curious. I became invested.

I have a friend who, at the time, recently became a millionaire in the insurance industry. I didn't call him to ask for money but to ask him for advice about money management. Together we went through a thorough financial analysis of how much money I was making versus how much I was spending monthly. To both of our surprise, I wasn't overspending, however, I wasn't making enough money to save. It was all being utilized. Every dime. Those big checks I was receiving from selling timeshares? They ran out. That job at

The Corona Cigar Company? I had to leave due to me catching bronchitis from the cigar smoke. My pockets were not happy. I was making enough money to pay my bills and feed myself. As a possible solution, he advised me to get a part-time job or search for another job that pays a better salary.

Ignoring God's guidance, and being scared to start being an esthetician and taking on real clients, I started thinking of little side hustles that would help me bring in extra money.

So I took my ass to the strip club to speak with the manager for the waitress position.

Immediately told me NO. And that was that.

However, while walking to my car from that embarrassing yet humbling experience, I heard a voice say "I have something better for you".

You see God gives guidance to his children through various means such as personal intuition, spiritual leaders, and prophets. Resisting this guidance is known as going against God's will and can result in various consequences. I didn't want to go against God, but just like most humans, I returned to my default system of panic instead of faith. But I knew

I had to change my response because I didn't want to feel stuck anymore and I didn't want to miss out on any opportunities God had for me. At that point, I had placed my safety, my sexuality, my finances, and my spiritual growth in the hands of God from that day forward.

The decision to place God in every area of my life was personal. Once again, He was my only option, I didn't have a boyfriend or Sugar Daddy to help me out. All I could do was depend on God.

During this time of my life, I began actively listening to inspirational podcasts. One day while listening, I heard the host mention that writing your goals down on a piece of paper or something that you can see every day will create clarity, accountability, and visualization to help you on your path to success.

That was life-changing for me.

Immediately I went searching for and found a black permanent marker, went into my bathroom, and started writing on my mirror. I started at the top with some simple things:

- Apply for health insurance and dental insurance
- Start a 401k,

- Save $230 a month for a downpayment on a house
- Workout 4 times a week
- Read 2 books a month
- Start my eyelash business

I also stopped watching reality TV. Yep! No more Love & Hip Hop and the Wendy Williams show. I wanted to eliminate all distractions that would hinder me from being great.

***

During this time, my daily routine became simple and focused:

Work out, eat, work, shower, watch tv

Work out, eat, work, shower, read a book

I was determined to try to read as many books as I could about my career and my character so that I could expand my knowledge and be transformed. I wasn't waiting for someone else to teach me anything because I was focused on my advancement.

That's how I stayed prayed up and un-fuck-with-able.

When you become focused, God will make things and people around be in a position to bless you.

While getting acquainted with my new position at Wyndham, I learned that the operations department consisted of a variety of computer systems, databases, and email communication that constantly flowed between the corporate office, the administrative team, and even the higher-ups. Even though I was kind of intimidated by the workload, the overall culture in the office was nice. Within a week or two of training, I was a professional in my position. Everything came easy to me...but I still needed to make more money.

Suddenly, there was a major leadership switch within the company that eliminated some higher-up positions which eventually led to a reassigning of management teams. Luckily for me, I was assigned to the best manager of all who later became an important part of my entrepreneurial journey. Her previous job title was the Director of Sales, and because of the reassigning and position eliminations, she became the Manager of the Administration Department, the Contracts Department, and the Accounting Department. As a result, she needed people around her to step up and show initiative; so I jumped at the opportunity and decided to introduce myself.

Nervous and excited, I took a vulnerable risk and let her know that I was having financial difficulties and that if I wasn't able to make more money I would have to get a part-time job or leave the company and find something that paid more. Her response was "There is overtime available, if you're willing to work you can have as much as you want".

To be completely honest, I knew she was sent there for me. She was invested in my development just as much as I was invested in growing within the company and making more money.

The difference between me and the other ladies in the office was that I was single with no children or pets. I had no outside distractions preventing me from getting to the money. My paychecks eventually doubled and my 14-hour workdays got me noticed by the higher-ups which eventually gave me personal access. Instead of communicating via email, I was invited to meetings and outings with the big dogs. That's when I started looking at the company as a paid apprenticeship.

My wardrobe got better, my language became more professional, I limited my association with office gossip, and as my confidence grew I started getting promoted to more leadership roles.

Soon after my manager began scheduling weekly meetings with me to work on building my brand within the company, email communication, and setting personal goals for my career. During one particular meeting, she asked me if I had a 401K. I explained to her that I did not, however, it was on my to-do list along with getting health and dental insurance. After spending an extra 2 hours in our meeting, I left work with a 401K with Merrill Lynch along with health and dental insurance with Cigna.

***

Training the new hires was a job responsibility that not only helped to develop my character and skill set but it also helped me to build my brand within the company. I particularly remember one new hire that came in and changed my life.

Due to us spending all of our time together during training, I learned that she was a single mom with two young sons. I also learned that she just left an airport management position because of a strict schedule that conflicted with her son's school schedule. She was looking for something more flexible and with a better salary.

I understood her needs because I came into this position with my own similar goals. I ended up sharing with her that I wanted to start my own eyelash business but I didn't know where to start.

Her response was, "That's easy, I can help you with that".

So during our 30 min lunch break, she helped me to apply for my LLC.

It was the easiest and best thing I've done. Beaming with excitement, I went home, got my marker, and started writing new goals on my mirror. I couldn't believe that the things I was writing in my mirror were coming true. I eventually learned that I was experiencing The Law of Attraction.

The Law of Attraction is a concept that suggests that your thoughts and emotions can influence your reality. What you focus on and put out into the universe will come back to you, in some way. Based on that notion alone, I started to accept the fact that I deserved to be happy, I deserved to be financially free, I deserved to find true love, and I deserve the finer things in life.

Here are the basic steps of how it works:

- Set your intention: This means deciding on what you want to attract into your life, such as a new job, a healthy relationship, or financial abundance.

- Focus on positive thoughts: This means visualizing yourself already having the thing you want and feeling grateful for it as if it has already happened.

- Take inspired action: This means taking steps that will bring you closer to your desired outcome. For example, if you want a new job, you might start networking or updating your resume.

- Believe in the outcome: If you don't believe it's possible, you will be less likely to take the necessary actions or emit the positive energy that the Law of Attraction requires.

- Trust God: This means letting go of any doubts or fears and trusting that God will work in your favor.

It's important to note that the Law of Attraction is not a guarantee, and there may be factors outside of your control that affect the outcome. However, many people believe that by focusing on positive thoughts, taking inspired action, and trusting God, they can increase the likelihood of achieving their goals.

It is also important to note that The Law of Attraction requires you to stay focused. You should be mindful of the company you keep and surround yourself with positive influences. The phrase "idle mind is the devil's playground" suggests that when people have nothing better to do, they may be more likely to engage in negative or harmful behaviors. This can be especially true for individuals who are single and have a lot of free time on their hands.

For us single ladies, it's important to stay active and engaged in positive activities, such as pursuing hobbies, learning new skills, volunteering, or spending time with friends and family. By doing so, you can avoid becoming bored or feeling unfulfilled, which can lead to negative thoughts and behaviors. Negative or toxic relationships tend to come about when there are feelings of loneliness or inadequacy. The key is to stay busy and be mindful of our thoughts and relationships so we can lead fulfilling and healthy lives.

***

After I applied for my LLC, it was as if God put a fresh battery in my back. I had a new sense of reality and I could feel that my dream was getting closer and closer. It's like I could taste it.

Can you believe I couldn't think past $10,000? Meaning, I thought that a $100,000 house was an extreme amount of money and there was no way I could ever save up the money to purchase such a thing by myself. But I remembered the fourth and fifth processes of the Law of Attraction,

believe in the outcome and trust the universe

So amongst all odds, I believed that I could do it. Hell, I had been saving money anyway, not even realizing what I was saving for. Once I saved the first thousand dollars, I was shocked. However, when I saved my first five thousand and then ten thousand, there was no stopping me. I saved fifty thousand dollars over two years. Along with actively working on my passion, my eyelash extension business.

The world was mine for the taking. There was nothing I put my mind to that I could not achieve. I was winning in every area of my life, everything that I touched prospered.

And just like that, I bought my first home at the age of 31, for $250,000.

Ephesians 3:20 says "Now to him who is able to do immeasurably more than all we ask or imagine, according to his power that is at work within us".

This verse emphasizes the greatness and power of God, who was able to do infinitely more than I could wrap my pretty little head around. It encourages me to have faith and trust God's power and allow Him to accomplish great things in my life.

I had to remind myself daily, "As a man thinketh in his heart, so is he." The moment you change your mind, nobody can hold you back.

100% THE PRETTY WAY

PRETTY

Recognizing the beauty and excellence in everything around you and within you.

Single & Pretty
Protip: Get Busy

INGREDIENTS:

Getting up and getting busy is essential for your physical and mental well-being. It's important because it helps us stay productive and accomplish more task, which can give us a us of accomplishment and satisfaction.

Recycle

| RELEASE ENDORPHINS | IMPROVE YOUR MOOD | SENSE OF PURPOSE | PERSONAL & PROFESSIONAL GROWTH | INCREASE SELF-CONFIDENCE |

CHAPTER 8:

Show up for life

Even in uncertainty and struggle,
keep showing up

(Bible Verse)
"Whoever heeds discipline shows the way to life,
but whoever ignores correction leads others astray"
-Proverbs 10:17

Now that my mind was focused and I was on the right path for my life, I had to do some self-realization.

"What is pretty?". That's the question I often asked myself. I spent quite some time learning the difference between being pretty externally and being pretty internally. I knew that I was a good person, however, I had a mean side as well. A defensive side that showed when I felt threatened or if someone stole from me. I eventually became tired of being so defensive. I was over letting what other people did to me dictate the way I was going to live my life. As a result, I became determined to get myself out of survival mode. However, to successfully do so, I realized I had a lot of healing to do from my childhood upbringing with my mother.

In 2014, I was a student at Norfolk State University (NSU) majoring in Exercise Science, and minoring in Kinesiology. It was my senior year and I only had

2 more internships and an exit exam to complete before I was eligible for graduation. Life was exciting and promising for me at the time because I was so close to obtaining my Bachelor's Degree. However, I was blindsided when I found out my mother was sentenced to 18 months in prison.

Due to her conviction, not only did her life change but so did mine. The student loans that I was receiving for tuition stopped immediately. Therefore, I had no funds to pay my tuition balance so that I could continue my final semester and no one to turn to for financial assistance; so I was forced to withdraw from the university and forgo my graduation and my degree.

I remember feeling so upset and embarrassed. As a result, I cut off all communication with my friends to avoid the "What happened?" and the "Where have you been?" questions. The thought of me explaining why I wasn't going to be at graduation was too much for me to face and eventually had me thinking and feeling as though I didn't deserve that part of life that I was so close to having. For as long as I can remember, there had been unforeseen things that would happen around me that sought to possibly destroy my willpower; I just figured this was just another one of those moments. So I just resolved that it was too good to be true for me.

My response? "Fuck it! What's next?"

Soon after, I met a lady who gave me the right amount of hope that I needed. She was a stand-in on a busy night at the club where I was waitressing and I was tasked to show her the ropes. By the end of the night, she approached me and said "I love your communication skills, have you ever sold timeshare?" I giggled and said, "Girl! The only thing I've sold is alcohol and food". She then proceeded to explain more about the timeshare business and to my surprise, I was interested. So we exchanged contact information and eventually scheduled an interview.

During the interview process, the recruiter mentioned that their flagship property was in Orlando Florida, and that was all the confirmation I needed to push me to the beautiful sunshine state. Just like I mentioned earlier in the book, I made a plan, got a second job, saved up for 6 months' rent, set a moving date, packed up my Honda Accord, and moved.

There I was a college dropout who was engaged to a narcissist, with a mother in prison, and feeling stuck and hopeless. However, God delivered the miracle that I needed which lit up a path for my next steps.

This is when the magic started happening. I had no clue where I was going to live in Orlando or if I was going to even get the job at Wyndham for the timeshare position. But for some reason, I knew I was going to be ok. So I broke off the engagement, pawned the ring, filled my gas tank, and headed to Orlando. It was a 10-hour drive from Suffolk, Virginia to Orlando, Florida, and I had never felt so energized and alive thus far. It was as if all of the street signs were giving me confirmation, the billboards were waving at me and to top it off, once I arrived the first phone call was from the recruiter in Orlando. She gave me the best news, there was a job fair happening in the next two days that I was invited to. Amazed with excitement and confusion, I had no idea what I was doing but, again, I knew I was going to be just fine, I just needed to get settled.

I stayed in a hotel for a few nights and eventually used Craigslist to find my first apartment. To my surprise, my credit was pretty decent and I was approved on the spot.

God, what did I do to deserve all the good that was happening to me?

I was indeed so grateful and feeling so blessed.

However, there was still the mom situation, that I couldn't avoid any longer. That was the first time in 10 years that my mom was restricted to one location with nothing but time to talk and figure things out. As for me, I was a Northern girl in a new city with no clue as to what she was doing and who needed her Mommy. During that time nothing else mattered, I was just desperate to be with, and even hear from, my mom again.

After time was served, God gave me my mom back. And she was perfect because she was the mom I knew. The mom I looked up to. My mom inspired and imparted to me the gifts of hair, makeup, lashes, and naturally being pretty. I got it all from her.

After her release, our daily phone calls consisted of prayer and discussing life decisions and goals. It was as if all the things I went through when I was younger were worth it for those exact moments for both of us to grow together...again.

You see, I was my mother's first-born child, she had me at the age of 15, therefore, we technically grew up together. I watched her go through all her stages in life; graduating from high school, getting her first apartment, having my siblings, dating, working, and making good choices and bad ones. Through it all, I never understood how my mother did everything. Yes, she had her struggles but I watched her raise three children, kept us all in the best clothing, always had a roof over our heads, and spoke positivity and God into our lives at the same time. Throughout my childhood, I never witnessed anyone who did it all like she did. She has always been the strongest woman I knew. Her resilience and determination were passed on to me and that is why we are the best of friends today.

I must say, it wasn't easy getting over years of hurt and disappointment. Family trauma can be tricky and difficult, however, if both sides are willing to put in the work to overcome the obstacles, miracles will form.

I witnessed my mom rebuild herself day by day. We both committed to each other to talk three times a week with healthy communication. While my mom was serving time, she was attending one-on-one counseling sessions, so it became natural for her to speak to me with the gentle voice of a healer instead of a patronizing one. It was as if she was now giving me all the answers and all the love I missed during those key years of my life. In those moments, my siblings and I had finally held the missing piece of the puzzle I'd been searching for in my life but never could find; a healthy mother-and-daughter relationship.

My siblings and I watched my mom transform her life before our very eyes. We watched her overcome being a single mom, she overcame a drug addiction and took accountability while serving her time in prison. Now I can confidently say that she is living her best life. All three of her children are alive and well, she is an active grandmother, she owns everything that she has, she goes to church every Sunday, and she is currently in a safe and loving relationship. This is why I gave her the title "The Strongest Woman I Know" because she lived a life that proves it.

Once our relationship was restored, we created a stronger, more healthy bond than I could have ever imagined. As a result of that relationship, all types of things were changing in other areas of my life, like understanding what real friendship was and knowing that all relationships should be healthy and reciprocal.

To all the ladies out there that have any kind of friction, unsettling feeling, or uncertainty about the relationship you have with your mother and/or daughter, invite God in and ask Him for help in that relationship. He will place forgiveness in your heart so that you can start the healing process of what could be the best relationship for both of yall lives.

Remember, nothing is done overnight, it takes time, patience, and effort to work through the trauma and build a healthier, happier relationship. Who would've ever thought meeting a stand-in lady in the club with a suggestion could lead to a new life, new journey, rediscovery, self-enlightenment, and blessed life full of abundance from God's glory?

100%  **THE PRETTY WAY**

Recognizing the beauty and excellence in everything around you and within you.

Single & Pretty Protip: Pursue your personal interest and hobbies

INGREDIENTS:

Personal interest and hobbies provide a much-needed outlet for stress relief, relaxation, & self-care, promoting overall well-being. They also help in building connections with like-minded individuals, expanding your social circle, and forming meaningful relationships.

 Recycle

| MAKES YOU MONEY | KEEPS YOU IN SHAPE | KEEPS YOU CREATIVE | SELFCARE | KEEPS YOU PEACEFUL |

CHAPTER 9:

Enjoy your peace and happiness

Trust Yourself

(Bible Verse)
"But the fruit of the spirit is love, joy, peace, patience, kindness, goodness, faithfulness, gentleness, self-control; against such things, there is no law"
- Galatians 5:22-23

Being single is fun and all, but on the other hand, this shit is for the birds. I am ready to find my man, my man, my man.

However, before I jump into another relationship, I couldn't help but ask myself...

Why?

What service will I be able to provide that man?

What advice would I give?

Am I in the right headspace for another breakup?

Am I in the right headspace to deal with someone else's mental issues?

I guess all women over the age of thirty at some point have to look at themselves in the mirror and ask themselves what they are living for and who are you living for. Until you can answer those two questions, you shouldn't even be thinking about dating or being in a relationship.

This got me thinking....

My journey of healing spiritually, physically, and mentally has granted me access to a newfound sense of peace, growth, and empowerment. I believe that God had me on this extended process to make sure that I fully embrace His strength and my resilience.

One thing I've constantly learned throughout this process is to trust in divine timing and surrender to the path laid out for me. It has allowed me to recognize my worth, by recognizing and embracing self-love and self-care as essentials for my life. This journey has also provided me with the opportunity to deepen my connection with others, as well as, foster empathy, compassion, and understanding. I would say the biggest advantage is that the entire journey has enabled me to fully step into my greatest potential and live a life guided by purpose and authenticity; that has been the most rewarding.

You see, I've done all this learning and maturing up until this point of my life to enjoy something more than just good conversations and great sex.

But God came to me one night and said "What if you removed sex from the equation and learned to lead with your mind, confidence, leadership, class, and charisma that I've placed in you?"

Wow, God you mean don't lead with being flirtatious, my sex appeal, and being promiscuous?

God replied, "Duh, use what I have placed in you and watch what happens."

So I paused and took a deep breath.

Then I started believing I could be that woman I've been searching for all these years. The Tiara God was recreating. It was me - I am her and that's when the idea of writing this amazing memoir came to mind. I needed to shed the old me so I could become the new me.

So what if I took sex out of the equation?

Will the guys still want to date me? Who the fuck cares!

My answer to that question is for me to be unapologetically me.

These past few years, I have built my self-esteem to a place that is unmatched by the average person. I have a strong sense of self-worth, I am confident in my abilities to have a great impact on younger women, and I am living a happier, more fulfilling life. And I will never let anyone take that from me.

When a woman has high self-esteem, it doesn't mean she is bougie or conceited. It simply means that she believes in herself and her abilities and potential. That she is more likely to be healthy, care about her self-image, can set boundaries, communicate effectively, and assert herself when necessary. She is also less likely to tolerate mistreatment or abuse, and more likely to seek out a partner who treats her with respect and kindness.

But sex is an important part of a healthy and fulfilling partnership, right?

First off, let me start by saying sex is good. Sex is a gift from God, that should be a sacred and loving expression of intimacy and commitment between a husband and wife; which is what I want.

A strong and healthy partnership should be built on a foundation of trust, mutual respect, communication, shared values and interest, and a relationship with God. I strongly think without these foundational elements, physical sex alone will not sustain the partnership.

However, I must admit, knowing that God created man and woman with these different sex organs has always confused me.

Like, why can a man orgasm easier than a woman? Why can't most women identify their G-spot while having sex? Why would God create such perfectly made human beings if it wasn't to explore and enjoy each other? These are the conversations I have with God, as it pertains to sex.

You see ladies, it is good to invite God into every area of your life, including your sex life.

As women, it is our right to know how our bodies operate. I've personally experienced and heard stories where a woman does not enjoy sex and feels like it's a chore for her. Well, let me tell you that knowing your own body and sexual preferences can lead to greater sexual confidence and assertiveness. When we understand how our body responds to stimulation, we can communicate our desires to our partners and advocate our sexual pleasure. And that's what I believe God is making me understand.

It's levels to this.

What I was previously experiencing sexually in the chapter "Celibacy" was out of the parameters of marriage. I was just creating soul ties with men who were not my husband and who were never destined to be my husband.

A soul tie is an emotional connection created during sex with two individuals that can be difficult to break. They can be positive or negative. A positive soul tie occurs between two people who have a healthy, loving relationship that is grounded in mutual respect, trust, and commitment. However, I was experiencing negative soul ties, in which two people engage in sexual activity outside of a committed relationship, leading to feelings of shame, guilt, and emotional distress.

Girl, it took me years to pray and repent so that those ties would break away from me. Thank God that they did!

Ladies, do not be ashamed of your past sexual experiences. As women, we tend to lose sight of the elegance of our presence due so easily to our past relationships and situationships.

Feeling ugly, tired, and stressed out all the time is a form of self-hatred or self-loathing. Which refers to having negative feelings or thoughts about yourself, feeling unworthy or undeserving of love and care, and having a lack of compassion and empathy towards yourself. The crazy thing about self-hatred is that it can manifest as you constantly focusing on your flaws and mistakes.

Going outside and looking crazy is not an attribute to being "pretty" ladies. Damaging your mental and emotional well-being, which then leads to feelings of depression, anxiety, and low self-esteem is the opposite of being "pretty". And we don't want that, trust me I've been there and done that. It's like a sunken place. It is hard to get yourself out of...but God!

With God anything and everything is possible. He will cultivate your life to its fullest potential, only if you're willing to build a relationship with Him and put in the work needed to have a healthy and fulfilling life.

With God, we have the power to create and attract anything we desire. A woman who is in her power is confident, self-assured, and empowered. She possesses a strong sense of self-awareness, understanding her strengths and weaknesses while being comfortable in her skin. She is assertive and knows how to communicate her needs and boundaries effectively. She is not afraid to say no when necessary and can stand up for herself without being aggressive or confrontational.

A woman in her power exudes confidence and radiates positive energy that inspires those around her.

She is resilient and views failure as an opportunity for growth. She has empathy for others and treats them with kindness and respect.

Again...She is me. I am her.

Now, seven years later I am more beautiful than I have ever been. I thank God for it all.

I purchased my first home and turned it into an eyelash and hair extension salon suite. I am a leader, a role model, and an inspiration to those around me. When people ask me why I'm single, I respond with:

"The partnership I'm praying for will be victorious. I seek a partner who is unbothered, strong-minded, truthful, a giver, respects himself, has a progressive relationship with God, has excellent people skills, and is wealthy. I pray for a fortified partnership where I'm able to trust his leadership."

And I know God will provide everything my heart desires.

Until then....I'll continue being Single & Pretty

100%

THE PRETTY WAY

Recognizing the beauty and excellence in everything around you and within you.

Single & Pretty Protip: Be Consistent

INGREDIENTS:

What you do every day matters more than what you do once in a while. Your daily habits have the power to change your life.

Recycle

POSITIVE HABITS   BUILD TRUST & RELIABILITY   ROUTINE   FOCUS BETTER   MOTIVATED

EPILOGUE

Interviews from my P.R.E.T.T.Y Ladies, as they share advice and affirmations to you my newest Pretty friend. I pray something is said that moves you closer to living life the pretty way!

Tiara:

Think about the younger you, what advice would you give your younger self?

What affirmation would you give the younger you, regarding singleness?

Kenea:

Advice - "You are MORE than enough." I'm reminding myself of this TODAY!

Affirmation - Follow your gut instincts. You will always take care of yourself if you just listen to yourself.

Signature - K.W.

NaNa:

Advice - You are young, you are beautiful, you are able. There are plenty of good men out there. Never stay in a situation too long thinking you will find better.

Affirmation - I am loved by me, I will not be confined to the wrong person, I will continue to attract happiness.

Signature - Nana T

Erika:

Advice - Save your money. Invest your money. Spoil yourself.

Affirmation - Learn yourself by yourself! Embrace and display your flaws (everyone has them)! Be patient, open to dating other races and learn other cultures.

Signature - Erika McDowell

Shalondra:

Advice - Always keep God first in my life and decision making. Get an education and career before children.

Affirmation - Always have standards and goals!! Stick to them!! But most importantly, love and respect me!! Never remain in any situation that does not honor me.

Signature - Bee

Cyndy:

Advice - Focus highly on my inner self and being true to myself. Making sure to always speak with God to lead me correctly. To think before acting and to remain humble in everything I do.

Affirmation - Always tell myself I am gorgeous no matter what. I am worthy of higher things and not to settle for whatever even if there is true love.

I will not pray and still worry.

Signature - Cyndy

Latoya:

Advice - I would tell my younger self it's ok to fail... failing means you tried. Failure gives you an opportunity to learn and grow... don't be afraid to fall because when you get up, you get up stronger.

Affirmation - "I trust myself" To make the right decision for my heart and my mind.

Signature - Toya

Sandy:

Advice - Be disciplined, more focused and not to be scared to cut what is not good out of my life.

Affirmation - "I'm whole, I'm beautiful, I'm a child of God. God is working on me to be ready for when my husband finds me. I will be ready for my husband to pour into me. I will continue to wear my singleness with pride and in a way, I honor the Lord."

Signature - S.Mangual

Loren:

Advice: Focus on you, build you, be proud of yourself and love yourself wholeheartedly

Affirmation: You are enough

Signature: Loren

Jasmine:
Advice:
1. The love I seek also seeks me.
2. My heart is open to give and receive love.
3. On the path to the person I am becoming, I still love the person I am.
4. You aren't alone, even if you feel alone.
Affirmation:
1. The love I seek also seeks me.
2. My heart is open to give and receive love.
3. On the path to the person I am becoming, I still love the person I am.
4. You aren't alone, even if you feel alone.
Signature: Evon

Jerina:
Advice: Live your life for you! Don't get into a relationship for the sake of being in one.
Affirmation: I love & respect myself!
Signature: Walk this way!

Molly:
Advice: I am enough! Be myself always. I don't need anyone or anything to feel better or whole.

Affirmation: I do what I love, I do what brings me passion and not worry about anyone else!
Signature: Molly Polson, Realtor

Tasha:
Advice: Be Latasha. Don't worry about it... enjoy the life that God gave you and make it your best. Don't stress about the small things, because this too shall pass.
Affirmation: I am worthy, strong, and self-sufficient and I don't owe anyone an explanation for my path, I can do all things through Christ.
Signature: Mrs. Jefferson

Feyrus:
Advice: Relax and focus on yourself. one thing you will never get back is time so don't waste your time. make wise decisions. Use every opportunity that comes on your way. learn from a mistake, put yourself first, set limits and boundaries, enjoy every moment no matter what. The ups and downs will pass and you will be just fine.
Affirmation: Don't chase anyone. protect your mind and heart. take your time, don't rush. a lot

of people will come in and out of your life. Set low expectations and accept what you can't change and have a lot of fun.
Signature: Fey

Janae:
Advice: -I would have just had a lot of fun and been fully present being single. I would have owned my singleness and embraced it if I had known I'd still be single in my thirties. I think desiring a relationship in my 20's robbed me of being present in the moment. There's so much fun having your freedom and it's worth being fully embraced until God brings the right person! Also, I would have trusted the Lord more. I didn't trust God to bring me the right guy.
Affirmation: Singleness is beautiful! It's a gift worth being treasured.
Signature: Ms. Schirle

Allison:
Advice: Stay true to your convictions and beliefs. Always be true to yourself as you are your own biggest supporter and advocate.

Affirmation: it's okay to not conform to society's predispositions on marriage and relationships. The natural progression of a relationship doesn't have to be marriage, house, kids. Sometimes things happen out or order, or not at all and that's okay

Signature: Allison

Tressa:

Advice: Life doesn't always give you what you want, but it gives you what you need.

Affirmation: No matter how hard life gets, get up and try again, and again, and again, and again, and again, and believe me it will get better.

Signature: Surviving Tressa

Samantha:

Advice: Time is timeless. Enjoy all the moments. Your time is valuable. Take nothing for granted. Don't ever hold back, Set boundaries and smart goals. It's okay to say no! Trust yourself with everything you always do. Ride the waves, that's what life's all about. Take the good with the good and the bad with the bad Learn to Chanel negative energy and know not everyone is on the same page or journey as you. And that's okay.

Affirmation: Your body is a temple. Treat yourself as nothing else. Enjoy yourself, love yourself more than ever, take time for you, get to know you. Keep falling in love with yourself repeatedly at the end of the day you know you best.
Signature: Samantha Krupa

Ariana:
Advice: I would tell younger me, patience and perseverance are key to success.
Affirmation: You are a talented, intelligent, and beautiful person. Don't ever stop being yourself!
Signature: Ari

Hope:
Advice: Don't let other people's vision of you be the person you create. I think the stigma around graduating high school, going to college, getting a masters, etc., is starting to become a thing of the past. Not everyone has a cookie-cutter fit to success, and just because your path to greatness looks different, doesn't mean it is wrong. I think a big thing we as a culture and society run into is not branding ourselves early on in life. Finding ways

to be creative and standout versus being just like 1,000 other girls is critical in becoming successful.

Affirmation: I think as I get older I realize how important faith and the family unit are in creating a home. Being single and finding yourself is a big part of that puzzle. If you are not happy on the inside, it will be much more difficult to find a compatible partner. If that means more time alone, then I think that is better than rushing in with the hopes to be married. Think of the bigger picture and find someone with common goals and aspirations.

Signature: Hope

Charlene:

Advice: Love yourself, enjoy life, know the difference between love and lust, know the difference between abuse in a relationship and love in a relationship, take advantage of educational opportunities, invest in your future, and know what the meaning of marriage is before you get married.

Affirmation: It's ok to say "No" and not feel guilty. It's not ok to let anger build up on the

inside. It's ok to release anger. It's not ok to "Keep up with the Joneses" and leave them alone.
Signature: My Granny

Melissa:
Advice: We are born with validation. So do not look for others to validate you.
Affirmation: You must have a relationship with God. God gives favor. You can not do life on your own.
Signature: Melissa Camper

Ashley:
Advice: These are the years that you are discovering how you envision the rest of your life and who you would like to spend it with. This is the time to have fun with family and friends while aligning what values are most important to you. Some of the best memories are going to come out of this chapter, so don't rush it and trust the process.
Affirmation: There is something magical about being independent. You are writing your own story and don't need anyone else to help you tell it. True love comes when you're least expecting and when you find the right person, you can still be the

independent younger you that you once were; just in different ways.
Signature: Ash M.

Domingue:
Advice: Don't Panic; everything is everything until it isn't.
Affirmation: You got this! You have no choice but to. Now figure it out.
Signature: D.G.P.P.

Liza
Advice: Remain yourself and don't compromise yourself for anyone. You are worthy of 100 percent unconditional love. When you love what you have, you have everything you need.
Affirmation: Good Vibes Only....REMAIN Focus, Persistent, Positive Purpose.
Signature: Lady Mystique

ABOUT THE
AUTHOR

Tiara Buster is a Muskegon, MI native, but currently resides in Orlando Florida. She is a lovable, energetic, genuine, and fun woman who loves God and his people! She has an affinity for seeing young women live and grow beyond their beautiful and pretty exterior, but live a life that exemplifies purpose resilience and edifying God every step of the way! Tiara is now a speaker, author, and beauty brand mogul, as a founder of the Shisopretty empire.

Connect with her, network with her, and join her as she continues to impact and inspire girls and women all over the world. showing them the way... The Pretty Way that is.

HIRE TIARA FOR YOUR NEXT EVENT

shisopretty | Instagram | Linktree

Presentation topics

Title: "The Power of the Pretty Way: Unleashing the Strength Within You"

Description: Good for conferences, leadership training, women empowerment. Dive deep into the heart of what it means to discover and embrace the inner strength of every woman. Using "The Pretty Way" as a guide, this presentation will not only empower women to realize their true potential but also inspire them to uplift others along the journey.

Audience Will Learn:

- The fundamentals of "The Pretty Way" and its transformative power.
- Practical methods for self-discovery and self-affirmation.
- Ways to combat societal pressures and redefine personal beauty and worth.
- The ripple effect of empowering oneself and its broader impact on the community.

Title: "Discovering Your Worth: Empowering the Youth for a Brighter Tomorrow"

Description: Good Schools, Colleges, Fairs, Youth Events, Private Conferences, In a world overflowing with external pressures, it's crucial for our youth to recognize their inherent value and worth. Tiara delves into the journey of self-discovery for young individuals, guiding them towards understanding and embracing their unique identities amidst societal noise.

Audience Will Learn:

- The importance of self-awareness and self-worth in the formative years.
- Tools and techniques to resist external pressures and redefine personal success.
- The power of positive self-talk, affirmations, and visualization in shaping one's future.
- Strategies for young individuals to set boundaries, honor their truths, and celebrate their unique journeys.

In Memory of Dana

In memory of Dana Fairbanks - My Best Friend of 15 years

When we think about the people who are most important in our lives, our best friends often come to mind right? These are the people who have been with us through thick and thin, who have laughed with us and cried with us, and who have always been there to offer a shoulder to lean on.

As we navigate through the ups and downs of life, it's important to have someone we can count on to share the journey with. Our best friends are often the ones who see us at our best and our worst, who know us better than anyone else, and who love us anyway.

One of the most beautiful things about a best friend is that they can be a constant in a world that is always changing. No matter what life throws at us, we know that our best friend will be there to support us. Whether it's celebrating our successes or helping us pick up the pieces after a setback, our best friends are the ones who stand by us through it all.

But having a best friend isn't just about having someone to lean on during tough times. It's also about having someone to share the good times with. When we achieve our goals or experience moments of joy, our best friends are often the ones we want to share those moments with. They are the people we turn to when we want to celebrate or when we just need someone to laugh with.

In many ways, having a best friend is like having a partner in crime. Together, we can take on the world and conquer our dreams. We can push each other to be our best selves and can hold each other accountable when we fall short. With a best friend by our side, we are never alone.

Of course, no friendship is perfect, and there will always be bumps in the road. But the beauty of a strong friendship is that even when we disagree or have a misunderstanding, we can work through it and come out stronger on the other side.

So as we go through life, let's cherish our best friends and the special bond we share with them. Let's be there in the same way that they are there for us. And let's never forget the power of having someone to share the journey with.

In conclusion, having a best friend who can go through life with us is a true gift. They are the ones who make the good times better and the tough times more bearable. So let's hold onto our best friends tightly and cherish the special bond we share with them.

I miss you, Dana.... Love you to the moon and back!!!!

ACKNOWLEDGMENTS

To my dear friends I left behind,

I want to share with you the reasons behind my actions. It was a matter of obedience. I felt compelled to distance myself from friends and family who did not share my faith in Jesus Christ. This decision was not easy, as it pained me to ignore phone calls and miss gatherings. However, I believed that God was working within me, and His plan required me to be surrounded by fellow believers, those who follow Jesus.

During this time apart, I was on a journey of growth and transformation. I needed to shield myself from the negativity and drain of the problems and lifestyles of those around me. This was essential for me to become spiritually stronger and deepen my love for Christ. I needed this separation in order to learn how to lead and inspire others in their faith.

I want you to understand that God is using me as a vessel for His people, and I am committed to not missing out on anything or anyone He has in store for me. If you feel that I have abandoned our friendship,

I want to sincerely apologize. My hope is that when you look at me now, you see the positive changes and growth that have taken place in my life. I pray that you see the presence of Jesus in me and upon me.

I give all the glory to God and invite His will to be done in me. In Jesus' name, I pray. Amen.

Tiara